Three Pillars of a Great Spiritual Leader

Charles Anthony

Greatness University Publishers
www.greatnessuniversity.co.uk

ISBN: 978-1-913164-56-0
ISBN-13: 978-1-913164-56-0

DEDICATION

To my wife Nadia who is one of the most influential Afro- American woman that has ever crossed my path. She has demonstrated a true form of Spiritual leadership and a complete dedication to the Gospel of Christ. Also, to all Spiritual leaders that have dedicated their lives to preach the great message of "King Jesus!"

CONTENTS

ACKNOWLEDGMENTS

This book has only been made possible because of the infinite wisdom of God. It has been a great privilege and joyous journey while writing this book. I have been challenged in my ventures of leadership. Hats off to all of those incredible leaders who have sacrificially allowed me a token of their wisdom. I am now indebted to each and every individual all over the country for their commitment to my vision.

I will like to express a special applaud to my friends and professors for their critiques in my ability to be a great leader. As a result, this long-awaited book is just the beginning of what is to come.

Lastly, a special thanks to my family members who are abroad that truly believed in my ability to be great. Also I cannot stop thanking my beautiful wife Nadia "Suga" Watson- Anthony and my kids for never giving up on me regardless of all the pleasures and pain we have experienced on this journey of togetherness. To all, "Be blessed on Purpose!"

Foreword

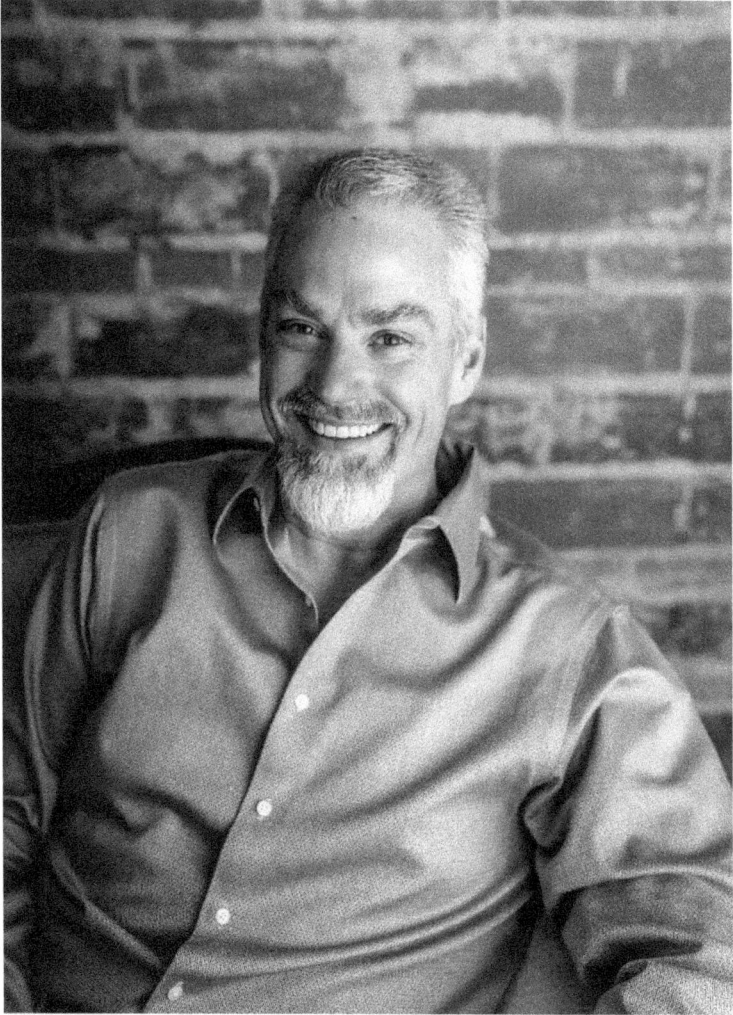

Ray Young
Entrepreneur
www.rayyoung.net

So much has been written on leadership, so why would someone write another leadership book? Primarily because so many leadership books are the same: based on theories and cliché comments that are challenging to actually put to work!

I am glad you have picked up this book. That is the first step. This book is different. It is not based on new ideas, theories or clichés. Charles Anthony is a man who has learned, applied and is writing about pillars of leadership that are tested, tried and proven from the earliest days of mankind.

You will be encouraged, equipped and inspired to make three great pillars the center point of your leadership. From the examples of Jesus, Moses, Queen Esther, Jonah, Deborah and more Charles does a masterful job of illustrating how these pillars of spiritual leadership are worked out in the lives of leaders.

One of the best things about this book is that Charles is not a researcher who writes theory. Charles has an incredible life story. His personal journey is inspiring and forms the background for how he discovered these pillars and the difference they make in real life. It has been my pleasure to know Charles as a friend in colleague for 5 years. I have personally seen him grow as a spiritual man and as a leader. Those really are not separate paths. As a person grows in the image of Christ they grow as a leader as well.

You have taken the first step. You purchased the book. Now read it. Highlight it. Reflect it. Apply it every day. Share the pillars with friends, family and colleagues. Make a difference in your life and in the lives of others!

On your marks, get set, GO!

Ray Young

rayyoung.net

Three Pillars of Great Spiritual Leadership

Introduction

Who invented leadership?

The key to Jesus' leadership was the relationship He had with the father. Man did not invent leadership. God did and He wrote a book about it, which He called the Bible. All of the answers to leadership are recorded in His word which is a manual of our Jehovah God leading man. We cannot separate the spiritual from the secular because God created man in his own image. Humanity was intended to be a spiritual being from the beginning and we were exactly that until the fall of Adam and Eve. Any existing human being remains spiritually dead until they are obedient to what the Bible says we have to do to become alive in Christ Jesus. It is at this point of obedience when man will become spiritually alive and should definitely live the character of Christ in their everyday walk until He returns.

What is Christian Leadership:

At the core of it, the phrase is somewhat an oxymoron. You may be asking, how? A person that humbles themselves to become a faithful servant today, is actually setting themselves up to become a leader tomorrow. Christian leadership is being willing to serve the greater good that demonstrates the willingness Serve, Sacrifice and Love God's way. It embraces the greater concept that expresses that meeting the needs of others is what allows churches, communities and businesses to reach their full potential of greatness. It involves going above and beyond to collaborate and achieve that which really does not have a direct benefit to yourself but an unfolding welcoming to embrace others even while considering the cost.

Jesus said in **Matthew** 20:26, 28, "It shall be so among you. But whoever would be great among you must be your servant, and whoever would be first among you must be your slave, even as the Son of man came not to be served but to serve, and to give his life as a ransom for many." Then Luke 22: 26, "But among you the one who serves best will be your leader."

These two versus are the foundation for Christian leadership. Jesus said the exact opposite of what the world says, as to the way a real leader is usually described. In the world, you would attempt to build some sort of self- absorbent attitude and you attempt to climb to the top. However, that is not the answer! "Jesus says, whoever serves best leads best." Servanthood is one true definition of leadership.

Leadership is not a matter of attempting to get people to serve your interest. Leadership is a matter if serving the best interest of others. Jesus says, if you want to be great you learn to be the servant of all. And as far as I am concerned there is no truer statement then this!

What is Spiritual leadership:

Spiritual leadership involves intrinsically motivating and inspiring workers through hope/faith in a vision of service to key stake holders and a corporate culture based on values of altruistic love to produce a highly motivated, committed and productive workforce.

Purpose of spiritual leadership:

Is to tap into the fundamental needs of both leaders and followers for spiritual well-being through calling and purpose; to create vision and value congruence across the individual, empowered team, and organization levels; and ultimately, to foster higher levels of employee wellbeing, organizational commitment, financial performance, and social responsibility.

A person's spirit is the vital principle or animating force traditionally believed to be the intangible, life-affirming force within all human beings who are obedient to God's word. (Acts 2:38) It is a state of intimate relationship with the inner self of higher values and morality as well as recognition of the truth of the inner nature of others. Today many individuals are struggling with what their spirituality means for their work since this is where they spend vast majority of their waking hours.

The office, being church or secular is now where more and more people eat, exercise, date, drop their kids, and even nap. Many naturally look to their organizations as a communal center because they lack the continuity and connection found in other settings such as the house of God. Moreover, recent acquirees have found that managers and leaders want a deeper sense of meaning and fulfilment on the job, even more than they want money and time off. And one of the primary ways to do this is by allowing the holy spirit to be a guiding light for us in any organization.

Because of this mind-set, a major change is taking place in the personal and professional lives of leaders as many of them more deeply integrate their spirituality and their work. Many agree that this integration is leading to very positive changes in their relationships and their effectiveness in the workplace environment. There are also statistics that workplace spirituality programs not only lead to beneficial personal outcomes such as increased job satisfaction, and commitment, but that they also improve productivity and reduce absenteeism and turnover. Employees who work for secular organizations they consider to be spiritual are less fearful, more ethical, and more committed in all areas in their lives. And, there is a scheme of evidence that a more humane workplace is more productive, flexible and creative. Most importantly for organizational effectiveness is the emerging research that that workplace spirituality could be the ultimate competitive advantage. Because of this, there is an emerging and accelerating call for spirituality in the workplace. This will open the door to being a more effective leader.

Workplace spirituality:

Is not about religion or conversion, or about accepting a specific belief system. Spirituality at work is about leaders and followers who understand themselves as spiritual beings who have a sense of calling that provides meaning and purpose for their lives. Men has always been the driving force of leadership in the church and secular environment. We have been titled with bread winner, head honcho, and guiding force of the work environment. However, as we look at the rising system of woman empowerment in today's world, they are becoming a lot more powerful and significant in all areas of leadership. In Jewish culture, women were accepted in all positions of leadership. And we find stories throughout the bible of woman who showed extraordinary leadership and courage.

Now as we go into this incredible exhortation on how to become a great spiritual leader, we will look into the lives of some of the most incredible men and woman leaders in all of humanity. Lets check our hearts while we do so!

"There is greatness within you. You just have to find its destination and take it on a Journey!"

Evangelist, Charles "Chuck" Anthony

Three Pillars of Great Spiritual Leadership

Service

Jesus' Service

Jesus submitted his own life to sacrificial service under the will of God (Luke 22:42), and he sacrificed his life freely out of the service for others (**John** 10:30). He came to service (**Matthew** 20:28) although he was God's son and was thus more powerful than any other leader in the world. He healed the sick (**Mark** 7:31-37), drove out demons (Mark 5:1-20), was recognized as a teacher and Lord (**John** 13:13), and had power over death (**Mark** 4:35-41; **Matthew** 9:18-26).

We are created to Serve others.

Ephesians 2:10 says, "For we are Gods workmanship, created in Christ Jesus for good works, which God prepared beforehand, that we should walk in them."

Long ago He planned that we should spend our lives in helping others. Even before we were born God planned a life of service for us, here on earth. Today there are so many people who are miserable because are missing a significant piece of their life. As we serve others, our own needs are met, and as we give our life away, we find it. Again, we are created to serve and if we are not serving we are missing out on one of the primary reasons we exist.

We are tested in our service, it proves that it belongs to Christ!

MOSES:

(A Leader tested by God)

Every leader, no matter the circumstance will eventually be tested in the work that he or she does. The task of leading the church or any organization for that matter, is not an easy road to walk. It requires a leader from every walk of life to be willing to face adversity and the testing of their character without being overcome by these testing's. It does not only take courage but it takes faith to resist these testing's that could hinder you from being Successful in any establishment. However, all leaders have to be willing to pay the price of greatness.

The great Moses is a prime example of these testing. He is definitely a leader's leader. He experiences great variations of testing. That would result in him saving God's people!

Moses commission:

Moses call to serve was his first test. Moses was out taking care of sheep in the desert, the angel of the Lord appeared unto him in a burning bush. When Moses was told by the Lord, "...I have indeed seen the misery of my people of Egypt and He told Moses I am sending you to bring my people the Israelites out of Egypt..." "Moses said unto God, Who am I, that I should go unto Pharaoh, and bring the Israelites out of Egypt?" (Exodus 3:10,11). After further discussion Moses accepted the call to be a servant of God. Leaders today are being tested by their response to God's directives to service.

Moses was also tested by going to an "unknown" people. The question arises, how would the people accept me, (a stranger) claiming to be someone who was sent by God to bring them out of oppression. However. With the help of God, he went in obedience and Moses was successful in this particular work.

In our world today leaders are also tested by the responsibilities that will take them to "unknown" places and persons as well. As a result, like Moses we must "GO!"

Moses problems:

Another, way that Moses was tested was in his confrontation with Pharaoh. Moses has to continuously go before the powerful leader Pharaoh who had a harden heart. This would be a great challenge to any man whether they are in leadership or not. Pharaoh attempted to try to get Moses to compromise concerning worship (**Ex.** 8:25, 28).

Pharaoh told Moses that he can take the people to worship but not outside. Moses did not compromise and he stood firm no matter the pressure. This is the lesson to any leader not to compromise the truth no matter the pressure that you are undergoing.

Moving forward, Moses had been tested by being challenged with an impossible task: the crossing of the Red Sea, (cf. 10:11, 24, 26). Can you fathom having to take on a task of this capacity with the enemy close behind. Leaders have to learn to stand firm in their faith and in their reasoning that God will be there to make it all possible. There were several other testing's that Moses had to encounter: the complaining of those who followed him, family members becoming jealous and ostracizing him, the sin and rebellion of the people, the people from the outside of his circle and not to mention the challenges he was receiving from the Lord or in some Leaders case those who has an influence on them as leaders.

Think about how overwhelming it is when you are trying to lead a rebellious people as Moses had done. This was a great deal of testing but the Lord said, "by this they will know that you are my disciples." By this he means when you love my people even when they are rebellious. As a leader of any organization you have to deal with various people of different walks of life. In this you are charged to organize, plan and guide others regardless of your biases, prejudices or subjectivity.

Moses faith and ability to lead was tested in every way you can imagine. This is an initiative to help us understand that our ability to lead will definitely be tested and we must continue to serve even when it hurt. Moses understood that his services was more important than his own selfish desires because that is the Spirit of a true leader!

Self-talk......

Are you being tested in your service in leadership?

Have you been more than willing to embrace the challenge?

_____

_____

_____

_____

_____

_____

_____

_____

_____

_____

_____

_____

_____

_____

_____

_____

_____

_____

_____

_____

_____

_____

Romans 7:4 says, "You are part of the body of Christ and now you belong to Him in order that we might be useful in the service of God." God says that the way you know that you are part of the body of Christ is that you serve others. Serving is the proof of our identity as members of His family.

We serve God by serving others

Queen Esther:

(The Leader of principles)

Esther is an inspiring story about a remarkable woman who was willing to risk her life to save her people.

She was a Jewish queen and a woman of principle, who was willing to put the lives of others ahead of even her own life. She was an outstanding example of serving others even under the most stressful circumstances. Jesus Christ said, "Greater love has no one than this, than to lay down one's life for his friends" **(John 15:13)**. Most of the time our lives may be pretty routine, but all of us have a few defining moments when we may be called on to put godly principle above personal benefit. Esther modeled bravery and courage when she risked her life to save the lives of her people.

Queen Esther showed great courage by telling the Persian king about a plan to assassinate him, and later, a plan to have all the Jews in Persia killed.

She teaches us that we must break intimidation and use our influence to bring glory to God. Leaders have to sometimes step out on the limb for those they are leading to show their willingness to serve. No matter how stressful circumstances may be as leaders we have to willingly exhort a courageous character.

Self-talk......

Are you demonstrating courage through your service?

Are you using your influence to bring glory to God?

_____

_____

_____

_____

_____

_____

_____

_____

_____

_____

_____

_____

_____

_____

_____

_____

_____

Colossians 3:23-24 says, "Whatever you do, work at it with all your heart as working for the Lord and not men. It is the Lord you are serving." No matter what you are doing, remember who are you doing it for? You are doing it for the Lord.

Matthew 25:40 Jesus said, "What you have done for the humblest of My brothers you have done for Me." He states positively, "If you have not fed and cloth others, then you feed and clothe me. If you have not clothed others, you have not fed and clothed Me." The greatest honour is to serve the Lord thy God.

Sacrifice

Jesus' Sacrifice

Paul writes, 'Therefore, I urge you, brothers and sisters, in the view of God's mercy [because of all that Jesus has done for us through the sacrifice of himself on the cross], to offer your bodies as living sacrifices, holy and pleasing to God,' (**Rom.** 12:1).

God wants you to offer all of yourself and all of your lives, your time, ambitious, possessions, ears, mouth and sexuality as well as your mind, emotions and attitudes. Paul's description of a living sacrifice also reminds us that you have to go on offering your life as a sacrifice to God, offering the whole of your life to fill the whole that is in your life.

We owe God everything!

Romans 12:1

Says, "Because of God's great mercy to us, offer yourselves as a living sacrifice to God dedicated to His service and pleasing to Him." The reason why I serve the Lord is because of what God has done for me because of His mercy. When I think of what Jesus Christ has done for me, there is no sacrifice that I can make for Him that will ever compare to what He has done for me.

Jonah:

A Leader that rejected responsibility

Every leader has an individual responsibility to God and to what they are called to do. Therefore, nothing is more fulfilling than to uphold our individual responsibilities before God! In order to be an effective leader we must meet the status quo of our responsibilities in all areas of our life. This is one of the most important qualities to have in the church of Christ or in any secular organization. In this day in age people are trying to place their responsibilities on others in order to avoid accountability. Most people that has the greater responsibility are doing just enough to get by. As a result, they take very few drastic measures to be successful and they have a "go with the flow mentality." This has contributed to a higher unemployment rate and dead dreams. Our nation has been totally affected by this dreadful mind set. Some look at the word (responsibility) as though the word itself is a Sin.

Statistically and factually we can see that not every church leader or those who call themselves leaders choose accept responsibility as they should. We can also base this on the grounds that Gods word demands certain actions out of leaders in the church.

From personal experience I have found it hard for church leaders to respond to simple questions such as, "who is responsible for...?" Just starting a statement with these small words cause the leaders to pose a defensive response. God demands us as leaders to take responsibility for our decisions even when ultimate Sacrifice is knocking at the door.

When you survey the Bible, you are able to see that there are several examples that show men and woman who rejects responsibility. As I was surveying the Bible one of the greater examples of God servant who rejected responsibility was the Leader and Prophet Jonah who served God among the Jews. Jonah was called upon by God to go and preach repentance to Niniveth, a wicked nation of about 600,000.

Jonah's Commission:

Jonah was instructed to go 500 miles to the East. There he would proclaim the destruction upon the Metropolis on the account of its wickedness. I am sure when Jonah heard this call, (**Jonah 1:2**) he must have surly thought God had made a mistake because he understood the risk. Jonah also knew that God would have forgiven them so became selfish of the cause. By the way at the time this was the largest Monarchy in the world. Therefore, this posed a great responsibility for just one man. Jonah would have loved to see them fall, however, he chose to take matters into his own hands and attempt to flee to Tarshish. In this attempt to flee the presence of God he went down to Joppa and paid a fee and boarded a ship that was going to Tarshish. (**Jonah 1:3**) As a result his irresponsible decision put others at risk, which was perversely counterintuitive.

Jonah's Problem:

Even though Jonah was a great prophet of God and a leader of Israel, he was not exempt from having some of the same problems of any mere man. Just like any leader there are certain responsibilities that are requested out of them that they do not want to uphold. Jonah seem to have encountered a big problem. He was not in favour of the command that God had given him. In today's world we call that "resignation." We as leaders would rather resign from a job or forfeit a task whether than take responsibility and tackle the task given to us. In the mind of humanity, fleeing or shirking responsibility is always the easiest way out.

Pride, was the first problem that Jonah was battling. Nineveh was an enemy was an enemy of God's chosen people and Jonah did not want to go there. To Jonah this would be humiliating to the Jewish mind. Pride is one of the sins in the bible that is mentioned that will cause you to receive condemnation from God. (**Obadiah 1:3**) Pride has destroyed great nations and the church. Therefore, we can truly expect for Pride to cause any small business organization or an up rise to any fortune five-hundred company to crumble when pride is the synergy of that leader.

Secondly, Jonah had an improper concept of God. At the root of shirking responsibility Jonah thought he could just say no and that would be the end of it. But it was not, there was still a responsibility that was required of Jonah. This was just the beginning! The lesson here is that as a leader we cannot just say "NO" action is required! When God tells a leader to do anything, it has to be done with no exceptions.

There were several other things that were problematic issues for Jonah, but there is one other that stood out to me. Jonah was willing to jeopardize the lives of others. The risk of being a leader could cause them to Sacrifice themselves but not at the expense of others. He was selfish and wanted things to be his way no matter the cost. This quality can destroy and company, city or individual. "But the Lord hurled a great wind upon the sea, and there was a mighty tempest on the sea, so that the threatened to break." A true leader knows that something has to be done. Even if that means taking total responsibility and make a sacrificial decision. Repentance and accountability are good for the soul and every leader one time are author when he does wrong!

Self-talk......

Are you causing the ship that you are controlling to go down?

Have you truly been Sacrificial as a leader?

_____

_____

_____

_____

_____

_____

_____

_____

_____

_____

Hebrews 13:16

Do not neglect to do good and to share what you have, for such sacrifices are pleasing to God.

It makes life meaningful!

Hannah:

Leader of Integrity

As strong woman that are leaders in all walks of life, you know what it means to sacrifice. Most woman give themselves, to daily devotions and applying their God given gifts to improve their time and self. When we survey the life of Hannah, we see an example of great sacrifice and a woman of great integrity. She experienced "losing" a child and disregarding one's own desires to give to another. Hannah was a woman with a great emptiness in her heart. That emptiness could only be filled by a child, a son for whom Hannah had longed for, for a long time. Hannah's husband, Elkanah, was a godly man. The Bible tells us in 1Samuel that, "Year after year he went up from his town to worship and sacrifice to the Lord at Shiloh." During this time of sacrifice, Elkanah gave portions of meat to his wife, Peninnah, and to all her sons and daughters. These were sons and daughters she bore to Elkanah. But to Hannah he gave a double portion because he loved her. It makes you wonder if Hannah had a "special" place in his heart? Could it be that they grieved together at not creating children from that love? It tells us in the Bible that, "the Lord had closed her womb." Here we see God's plan as it unfolds and how he had a very specific purpose in not willing blessings to Hannah and Elkanah until the precise time. This is to confirm to us that no matter how we want a process to be in the Christian or Secular world, it all has to happen in God's timing. Peninnah had used Hannah's barrenness against her and wielded her influence purposefully in badgering and hurting Hannah. This exhaustion of pain went on year after year. I believe that Peninnah did this behind her husband's back. Hannah, being of a meek and quiet spirit did not want to gossip or display the same hatred toward Peninnah. So, she did not convey to her husband what had transpired and the situation continued without any investigation. Elkanah would say to Hannah, "Why are you weeping? Why don't you eat? Why are you downhearted?" It was clear that Elkanah had no awareness of the torment Peninnah was yielding towards Hannah. Holding onto this torment and not sharing it with her husband was another way in which she gave sacrificially.

She did not want to show any disrespect to the other woman because of her love for Elkanah. Surely, he was quite aware of the grief of carrying an empty womb as he said to her, "Don't I mean more to you than ten sons?" I am sure that this question was one that was bitter sweet. I can feel the quenching heart

Hannah must have felt at that moment. She was bitter that she had never nurtured a baby at her breast, bitter at the pure emptiness of her barren womb. On the other hand, sweetness, in that her husband had wanted her to adore only him, to see him as fulfilling her needs, and in the deep love the two of them shared.

Hannah remained steadfast through her trials and maintained her integrity as any leader should do, but things came to a head during one particular time while they were in Shiloh.

It was there that Hannah let it all be revealed. Eli, a priest at the temple door, saw Hannah weeping bitterly and praying out to the Lord. At this point she made a vow saying, "O, Lord Almighty, if You will only look upon your servant's misery and remember me, and not forget your servant, but give her a son, then I will give him to the Lord for all the days of his life, and no razor will ever be used on his head. As she prayed silently only moving her lips, Eli thought she was drunk and said to her, "How long will you keep on getting drunk? Get rid of your wine!" Hannah replied that she was not drunk, but a woman of a sorrowful spirit.

Sometimes the way a leader handles a situation will be misunderstood. However, as you expose your vulnerability, this is an objective way to maintain your integrity.

I believe that Hannah was consumed before the pouring out of her spirit that day, and that it was in the very act that Hannah was able to find peace. Eli answered and told her to go in peace and blessed her petition. It was then that Hannah left with a renewed joy in her heart. She was able to eat and had a smile upon her face. It was the act of "giving it" to the Lord that brought renewal.

The next morning, they rose early and worshipped the Lord and returned to their house in Ramah and the Bible says that, "Elkanah knew his wife". I love the use of the word "knew" here, as it shows the beauty of the intimacy that they shared together.

Imagine the relief that Hannah could now have in her marriage bed with her precious husband without the joy robbing her of the worry of not bearing a child. The influence of worry no longer was an umbrella to the love she shared with him. She had given it to the Lord and placed it in His will in fully capable hands.

In due time the Lord blessed Hannah with a son and she named him Samuel. Samuel's name means, most fittingly, "For this child I prayed." The time had come once again that Elkanah took his whole house to offer his yearly sacrifice and his vow. Hannah stayed behind, for she said unto her husband, "I will not go up until the child is weaned and then I will bring him that he may appear before the Lord and remain there forever." Elkanah told her to do what she thought was right and keep Samuel until he was weaned. So, Hannah continued nursing her son until the time came. Hannah kept her promise to the Lord and gave Samuel back as a sacrifice of her obedience. Hannah took Samuel to the house of the Lord in Shiloh and the Word says that Samuel grew and worshiped the Lord there. All leaders have those hard decisions to make and in the process of those decisions they are to maintain their integrity. Due to Hannah's integrity and commitment she was blessed by God!

In **1 Samuel** 2, you can read Hannah's beautiful prayer of praise. Hannah is a lovely woman of integrity. In her we see a determined woman who believed in a God that was bigger than a barren womb. She was a woman who knew to pour and empty herself out to the Lord and to leave burdens with him. She knew where to go and where to find peace. She was a woman who gave of her first fruits—the child of her womb.

How can you learn from Hannah's example?

Most of us have given sacrificially for our children, our Job's and our life at one point or another. When you a woman of integrity your business is affected by this outstanding attribute. It does not matter whether our sacrifice is big or small, God sees it. He is still a God that answers prayers and will bless you according to his riches and glory!

Self-talk...

Are you a woman of sacrifice?

Are you a woman of influence?

Are you a woman of integrity?

_____

_____

_____

_____

_____

_____

_____

_____

_____

Love

Jesus' Love:

The perfect expression of God's love for us is found not only Jesus' love for us but also in the person of Jesus. Jesus did not require anything out of anyone that he did not live out on His own. The command to love one another (John 13:34), and love for our neighbors as ourselves (Matthew **22:39)** was first demonstrated by Jesus and then command of His followers.

Jesus' love was expressed through His compassion of others. He was the most incredible example of a leader with a perpetual love that is undefined. Let's love others with the love of God.

God is holy and loving. God loved David. He said, 'I will not take my love from him. God, in his love, made a covenant with David and his people. It was a covenant of grace, but it required a response of obedience to the law. But what would happen if they did not keep the law? 'If his sons forsake my law and do not follow my statutes, if they violate my decrees and fail to keep my commands' (Ps. 89:30–31) – a penalty would be required (v.32).

The New Testament tells us that God came in the person of his son Jesus Christ to take that penalty by offering himself as the sacrifice for sin. Through that sacrifice, God's love and holiness were both fully expressed and satisfied and now we are free indeed!

Our love will be rewarded in eternity.

1 Corinthians 13:4-5

Love is patient, love is kind. It does not envy, it does not boast, it is not proud. It does not dishonor others, it is not self-seeking, it is not easily angered, it keeps no record of wrongs.

If the love of God as shown in Christ Jesus is not enough to convince you of His love for you, here is an individual in the Bible who, after experiencing the relentless love of God, testify that His love really is incomparable.

David:

A Leader after God's own heart

Many Christians in the world today love David. During the time before he became king, however, David was no more than a shepherd boy who loved to take care of his father's sheep. When we think about his story, we notice that his family did not really give much attention to him: his father seemed ashamed of him, opting to present him to the prophet

Samuel as a last option (**1 Samuel** 16:11); while his brothers looked down on him or were perhaps insecure of him. (**1 Samuel** 17:26-31)

David, however, knew that God loved him. His experiences with God enabled him to defeat Goliath, become Israel's most-loved king, and write one of the most beautiful declarations a God-fearing man could ever say:

> *"O Lord, our Lord, how excellent is Your name in all the earth! You have set Your glory above the heavens. Out of the mouth of babes and nursing infants You have ordained strength because of Your enemies, to silence the enemy and the avenger. When I consider Your heavens, the work of Your fingers, the moon and the stars, which You have established, what is man that You are mindful of him, and the son of man that You attend to him?"* (**Psalm** 8:1-4)

David's tragedies in leadership:

King Saul became jealous of David's success. David was forced to flee to and live the life of an outlaw until the death of Saul (**1 Sam.** 19:11; 21:11/19-25:1).

David committed adultery with Bethsheba who became pregnant (**2 Sam.** 11:4-11:5).

David arranged the death of Bathsheba's husband

Uriah (**2 Sam.** 11:17).

David confessed and repented his sin and God forgave him, but Bethsheba's child died (**2 Sam.** 12:10, 13, 19).

David failed to discipline his sons. His son Amnon committed sin of rape and incest; He was murdered by David's son Absalom (**2 Sam.** 13:14-29).

David son Absalom led a rebellion in an attempt to usurp David's throne (**2 Sam.** 16-17).

David's "beloved son" Absalom was murdered and David's throne was restored. It was a bitter victory for a heart-broken father (**2 Sam.** 18:14,15).

This is just to name a few. But as we know when we are embracing leadership with the mind of Christ; then God will turn those Trails into Triumphs!

David's Triumphs in Leadership:

God anointed David king of Israel when he was a boy. He defeated Goliath, married King Saul's daughter and became a hero in Saul's army (**1 Sam** 16:1-13; 17:1-58; 18:20-30).

David became king of Judah and then king of the united 12 tribes of Israel (**2 Sam.** 2:4).

Davis conquered Jerusalem (**2Sam**.5).

God promise David that his throne will last forever (**2Sam**. 7:16; 23:5; 1Chr 17:16-27; 2 Chr.13:5).

God called David "a man after God's own heart" (**1 Sam**. 13:14)

David anointed his son, Solomon, King of Israel (**1Kings** 1:28-40).

It was the beginning of the Davidic dynasty that reached fulfilment in Christ the King (**Mt**. 1:1; **1 Tim**. 6:14-15)!

We are charged as leaders in all areas of leadership to maintain our devotion to those around us even if man do not see who you called to be. There will be an ultimate promotion that only comes down from heaven. It is important to be willing to fall in love with what we have been called to do in our leadership positions.

The Bible regards David as the model king of Israel, and the books of Samuel, Kings, and Chronicles describe his many successes. Yet even David, "a man after God's own heart"(1 Sam.13:14), abuses his power and acts faithlessly at times. He tends to succeed when he does not take himself too seriously, but gets into serious trouble when power goes to his head—for example when he takes a census in violation of God's command (2 Sam. 24:10-17) or when he sexually exploits Bathsheba and orders the assassination of her husband, Uriah (2 Sam. 11;10-17). Yet despite David's failings, God fulfills his covenant with David and treats him with mercy.

This mercy that was given to David is a free gift from God but is received in different measurements according to their purpose. Therefore, leaders are not encouraged to take advantage of God's grace, by taking their earthly positions for granted. But we are encouraged to maintain grace in a manner that is worthy to God.

Self-talk...

Are you truly searching your heart to determine whether or not every beat is steadfast on God's desire for you?

Are you a man after Gods own heart?

Take a moment to deeply evaluate these questions and answer them.

_____

_____

_____

_____

_____

_____

_____

_____

_____

_____

_____

_____

_____

_____

_____

Proverbs 3:3-4

"Let love and faithfulness never leave you; bind them around your neck, write them on the tablet of your heart. Then you will win favor and a good name in the sight of God and man.

Love: Love is limitless

(Judge) Deborah:

A Distinguished Leader:

Deborah (Hebrew, "bee") appears to have been a homemaker at the time she is selected for service to her country. Having no aristocratic lineage, she is identified simply as "the wife of Lappidoth." Yet Deborah was the only woman in Scripture elevated to high political power by the common consent of her peers.

Though her homemaking responsibilities may have well taken a backseat during her service to her country, she described herself as "a mother in Israel" (**Jud**. 5:7) before she became a judge. This could be a reference to her own offspring or an expression of her spiritual motherhood toward every son and daughter of Israel.

In spiritual stricken Israel, characterized by rejection of God and a determination for each to do things her own way (**Jud**. 17:6; 21:25), Deborah displayed her leadership first as a counselor discussing and suggesting solutions to people with problems near her home. The civil court system was inept; the military was too weak to defend national borders; the priesthood of what had been a theocracy was impotent and ineffective. Normal life was no longer possible. And thus, Deborah rose to become a judge and eventually, a deliverer of her people in time of war.

God had spoken in the past through his leaders Moses and Joshua, and now he was speaking through Deborah. In a slight reflection of the crossing of the Red Sea, the horse-drawn chariots of the enemy floundered and Yahweh came to her aid with a violent thunderstorm (**Jud**. 5:4). The destruction of the Canaanite power was immortalized in one of the finest specimens of Hebrew poetry by Deborah and Barak, as they picture in a song of praise the events which led to victory for the people (**Jud.**5).

Long before Deborah exercised her uncommon leadership and decision making skills to save her nation in a time of trouble, she was a homemaker, a wife and mother in Israel. Her compassion had been awakened by the atrocities suffered by her people. She arose to make herself available, and she was victorious as she herself trusted God, loved God and then inspired others within her sphere of influence with that same trust and love. Leaders have to be available and willing to have an encounter with the Lord. This demonstrates that you have the ability to lead others in the most uncommon way. In a way that results in prosperity.

If you evaluate Deborah's life you can see that her love for God propelled her to a place that was unbelievable. She got what a leader deserved; a position that only God can give her. Why? Because she knew her place! I want to encourage those who feel that they are just stay at home moms. This does not mean that God is absent or you are unworthy. If you are willing and are determined to limitlessly pour your love into Christ, you can conceive the power to rule a nation.

Wives, Mothers, and Daughters of God know your worth, and do not take for granted the power given to you by God! Remember true greatness is on the inside that was given to you before the existence. You just have to dig deep to find it.

Self-talk....

Woman of God do you know your worth?

If so, what is it?

_____

_____

_____

Three Pillars of Great Spiritual Leadership

Great Spiritual Leadership:

Is a *Service* that employs *sacrificial love*!

Evangelist, *Charles "**Chuck**" Anthony*

The bible teaches that the sacrificial life and death of Jesus not only provides salvation, impels us towards sanctification, but also inspires us to reflect God's sacrificial; love to others (**2 Cor.5:14, Rom. 8:35-39)**. Frankly, we are aware that our service and sacrificial love is the farthest thing from our hearts.

"10 Spiritual Leadership principles"

1. Understand what is your responsibility and what is God's responsibility.
2. Maintain the three abilities of leadership; Vulnerability, responsibility and possibility.
3. Maintain a self-awareness
4. Spiritual insight into the heart of others
5. Understand faith
6. Encourage Truth
7. Godly courage
8. Discerned vision
9. Sensitivity to Self-Awareness
10. Embrace Godly attributes such as Service, Sacrifice and Love

Self-talk

What spiritual principles do you aquire?

Do you actually use them towards spiritual growth?

_____

_____

_____

_____

_____

_____

_____

_____

_____

_____

_____

_____

_____

_____

_____

_____

About the Author

Charles Anthony is a brilliant son, an incredible father and a devoted husband. He is from the mean-stricken streets of Fort Worth TX. Where life defined you by poverty and status. After years of hardship Charles managed to elevate above his circumstances and own his purpose. As a result, Charles has gone on to become an Evangelist at Sidney Church of Christ. He has a (Bachelors degree in biblical studies) from Sunset bible institute. Charles is a reoccurring student at Sunset Bible institute to achieve his (Masters in Spiritual Leadership).

Charles is a certified Fitness and Nutrition coach. He is a certified distributor for Herbalife nutrition with Online store- (Armor-fitbizz). Charles is a Certified Marriage counselor through pre-pare enrich. Charles is a Certified Satellite bible school instructor. He is a Certified New Life Behavior instructor- (prison ministry) and has also successfully completed Toastmasters international, which acquired him the skills of a Motivational speaker.

Serving in his community Charles wrote inspirational article for San Saba newspaper in San Saba, Texas. Currently Charles is writing monthly inspirational articles for Sidney Herald Newspaper in the state on Montana. Charles has Co- authored several of books, "Les Brown changed our lives, Jesus changed our live," (The book of love) "How to love God's way."

Charles is also a mentor for "Christian Maturity for teenagers." Charles loves to serve people and most of all his lord and savior Jesus Christ.

Three Pillars of Great Spiritual Leadership